PENGUIN CLASSICS

THE ART OF WAR

Little is known for definite about Sun-tzu (544–496 B.C.) and his life during the Warring States period after the decline of the Zhou dynasty, but his classic *The Art of War* had been one of the central works of Chinese literature for 2,500 years.

John Minford has translated many books from Chinese, include Cao Xueqin's *The Story of the Stone*, and was co-editor of *Seeds of Fire: Chinese Voices of Conscience* and *Chinese Classical Literature: An Anthology of Translations*.

PENGUIN (✿) CLASSICS

THE ART OF WAR

Little is known of Sun Tzu beyond his name, Sun Wu, and his role during the Warring States period, when the *Art of War* was composed, but the classic treatise he left behind remains the central work on the art of warfare for East Asia.

John Minford has translated many books for Penguin, including the *Analects*, *The Story of the Stone*, and a companion volume to the *Tao Te Ching*, *I Ching* and *Art of War* (forthcoming).

SUN-TZU

The Art of War

Translated by
JOHN MINFORD

PENGUIN BOOKS

PENGUIN CLASSICS

Published by the Penguin Group
Penguin Books Ltd, 80 Strand, London WC2R 0RL, England
Penguin Group (USA) Inc., 375 Hudson Street, New York, New York 10014, USA
Penguin Group (Canada), 90 Eglinton Avenue East, Suite 700, Toronto, Ontario, Canada M4P 2Y3
(a division of Pearson Penguin Canada Inc.)
Penguin Ireland, 25 St Stephen's Green, Dublin 2, Ireland
(a division of Penguin Books Ltd)
Penguin Group (Australia), 250 Camberwell Road, Camberwell, Victoria 3124, Australia
(a division of Pearson Australia Group Pty Ltd)
Penguin Books India Pvt Ltd, 11 Community Centre,
Panchsheel Park, New Delhi – 110 017, India
Penguin Group (NZ), 67 Apollo Drive, Rosedale, North Shore 0632, New Zealand
(a division of Pearson New Zealand Ltd)
Penguin Books (South Africa) (Pty) Ltd, 24 Sturdee Avenue, Rosebank, Johannesburg 2196, South Africa

Penguin Books Ltd, Registered Offices: 80 Strand, London WC2R 0RL, England

www.penguin.com

A portion of this translation first appeared in *The New England Review*
First published in the United States of America by Viking Penguin 2002
Published in Penguin Classics 2008

027

Translation copyright © John Minford, 2002
All rights reserved

The moral right of the author has been asserted

Set by Rowland Phototypesetting Ltd, Bury St Edmunds, Suffolk
Printed and bound in Great Britain by Clays Ltd, Elcograf S.p.A.

978-0-140-45552-6

www.greenpenguin.co.uk

Contents

Making of Plans

Master Sun said:

> War is
> A grave affair of state;
> It is a place
> Of life and death,
> A road
> To survival and extinction,
> A matter
> To be pondered carefully.

There are Five Fundamentals
> For this deliberation,
> For the making of comparisons
> And the assessing of conditions:
> The Way,
> Heaven,
> Earth,
> Command,
> Discipline.

The Way
> Causes men
> To be of one mind
> With their rulers,

To live or die with them,
And never to waver.

Heaven is
   Ying and Yang,
   Cold and hot,
   The cycle of seasons.

Earth is
   Height and depth,
   Distance and proximity,
   Ease and danger,
   Open and confined ground,
   Life and death.

Command is
   Wisdom,
   Integrity,
   Compassion,
   Courage,
   Severity.

Discipline is
   Organization,
   Chain of command,
   Control of expenditure.

Every commander is aware
   Of these
   Five Fundamentals.
   He who grasps them

Wins;
He who fails to grasp them
Loses.

For this deliberation,
For the making of comparisons,
And the assessing of conditions,
Discover:

Which ruler
Has the Way?

Which general
Has the ability?

Which side has
Heaven and Earth?

On which side
Is discipline
More effective?

Which army
Is the stronger?

Whose officers and men
Are better trained?

In which army
Are rewards and punishments
Clearest?

From these
    Can be known
    Victory and defeat.

Heed my plan,
    Employ me,
    And victory is surely yours;
    I will stay.

Do not heed my plan,
    And even if you did employ me,
    You would surely be defeated;
    I will depart.

Settle on the best plan,
    Exploit the dynamic within,
    Develop it without,

Follow the advantage,
    And master opportunity:
    This is the dynamic.

The Way of War is
    A Way of Deception.

    When able,
    Feign inability;

    When deploying troops,
    Appear not to be.

When near,
Appear far;

When far,
Appear near.

Lure with bait;

Strike with chaos.

If the enemy is full,
Be prepared.
If strong,
Avoid him.

If he is angry,
Disconcert him.

If he is weak,
Stir him to pride.

If he is relaxed,
Harry him;

If his men are harmonious,
Split them.

Attack
Where he is
Unprepared;
Appear

Where you are
Unexpected.

This is
Victory in warfare;
It cannot be
Divulged
In advance.

Victory belongs to the side
That scores most
In the temple calculations
Before battle.
Defeat belongs to the side
That scores least
In the temple calculations
Before battle.
Most spells victory;
Least spells defeat;
None, surer defeat.
I see it in this way,
And the outcome is apparent.

Waging of War

Master Sun said:

In War,
>   For an army of
>   One thousand
>   Four-horse swift chariots,
>   One thousand
>   Hide-armoured wagons,
>   For one hundred thousand
>   Mail-clad soldiers,
>   With provisions for
>   Four hundred miles;
Allowing for
>   Expenses at home and at the front,
>   Dealings with envoys and advisers;
>   Glue and lacquer,
>   Repairs to chariots and armour;
>   The daily cost of all this
>   Will exceed
>   One thousand taels of silver.

In War,
>   Victory should be
>   Swift.
>   If victory is slow,

Men tire,
Morale sags.
Sieges
Exhaust strength;
Protracted campaigns
Strain the public treasury.

If men are tired,
Morale low,
Strength exhausted,
Treasure spent;
Then the feudal lords
Will exploit the disarray
And attack.
This even the wisest
Will be powerless
To mend.

I have heard that in war
Haste can be
Folly
But have never seen
Delay that was
Wise.

No nation has ever benefited
From a protracted war.

Without a full understanding of
The harm
Caused by war,

8

It is impossible to understand
The most profitable way
Of conducting it.

The Skilful Warrior
        Never conscripts troops
        A second time;
        Never transports provisions
        A third.

        He brings equipment from home
        But forages off the enemy.
        And so his men
        Have plenty to eat.

Supplying an army
        At a distance
        Drains the public coffers
        And impoverishes
        The common people.

Where an army is close at hand,
        Prices rise;
        When prices rise,
        The common people
        Spend all they have;
        When they spend all,
        They feel the pinch of
        Taxes and levies.

Strength is depleted
>On the battlefield;
>Families at home
>Are destitute.

The common people
>Lose seven-tenths
>Of their wealth.
>Six-tenths of the public coffers
>Are spent
>On broken chariots,
>Worn-out horses,
>Armour and helmets,
>Crossbows and arrows,
>Spears and bucklers,
>Lances and shields,
>Draft animals,
>Heavy wagons.

So a wise general
>Feeds his army
>Off the enemy.
>One peck
>Of enemy provisions
>Is worth twenty
>Carried from home;
>One picul
>Of enemy fodder
>Is worth twenty
>Carried from home.

The killing of an enemy
    Stems from
    Wrath;
The fighting for booty
    Stems from
    A desire for reward.

In chariot fighting,
    When more than ten
    Enemy chariots are captured,
    The man to take the first
    Should be rewarded.
Change the enemy's
    Chariot flags and standards;
    Mingle their chariots
    With ours.

Treat prisoners of war kindly,
    And care for them.
    Use victory over the enemy
    To enhance your own strength.

In War,
    Prize victory,
    Not a protracted campaign.

The wise general
    Is a Lord of Destiny;
    He holds the nation's
    Peace or peril
    In his hands.

Strategic Offensive

Master Sun said:

In War,
    Better take
    A state
    Intact
    Than destroy it.

Better take
    An army,
    A regiment,
    A detachment,
    A company,
    Intact
    Than destroy them.

Ultimate excellence lies
    Not in winning
    Every battle
    But in defeating the enemy
    Without ever fighting.
    The highest form of warfare
    Is to attack
    Strategy itself;

The next,
> To attack
> Alliances;

The next,
> To attack
> Armies;

The lowest form of war is
> To attack
> Cities.
> Siege warfare
> Is a last resort.

In a siege,
> Three months are needed
> To assemble
> Protective shields,
> Armoured wagons,
> And sundry
> Siege weapons and equipment;
> Another three months
> To pile
> Earthen ramps.

The general who cannot
> Master his anger
> Orders his troops out
> Like ants,
> Sending one in three
> To their deaths,

Without taking the city.
This is the calamity
Of siege warfare.

The Skilful Strategist
　　Defeats the enemy
　　Without doing battle,
　　Captures the city
　　Without laying siege,
　　Overthrows the enemy state
　　Without protracted war.

He strives for supremacy
　　Under heaven
　　Intact,
　　His men and weapons
　　Still keen,
　　His gain
　　Complete.
　　This is the method of
　　Strategic attack.

In War,
　　With forces ten
　　To the enemy's one,
　　Surround him;
　　With five,
　　Attack him;
　　With two,
　　Split in half.
　　If equally matched,

Fight it out;
If fewer in number,
Lie low;
If weaker,
Escape.

A small force
    Obstinately fighting
    Will be captured
    By a larger force.

The general is the prop
    Of the nation.
When the prop is solid,
    The nation is strong.
When the prop is flawed,
    The nation is weak.

A ruler can bring misfortune
    Upon his troops
    In three ways:

    Ordering them
    To advance
    Or to retreat
    When they should not
    Is called
    Hobbling the army;

Ignorant interference
In military decisions
Confuses
Officers and men;

Ignorant meddling
In military appointments
Perplexes
Officers and men.

When an army is confused and perplexed,
The feudal princes
Will cause trouble;
This creates
Chaos in the ranks
And gives away
Victory.

There are Five Essentials
For victory:

Know when to fight
And when not to fight;

Understand how to deploy
Large and small
Numbers;

Have officers and men who
Share a single will;

Be ready
For the unexpected;

Have a capable general,
Unhampered by his sovereign.

These five
   Point the way to
   Victory.

Hence the saying
   'Know the enemy,
   Know yourself,
   And victory
   Is never in doubt,
   Not in a hundred battles.'

   He who knows self
   But not the enemy
   Will suffer one defeat
   For every victory.

   He who knows
   Neither self
   Nor enemy
   Will fail
   In every battle.

Forms and Dispositions

Master Sun said:

Of old,
    The Skilful Warrior
    First ensured
    His own
    Invulnerability;
    Then he waited for
    The enemy's
    Vulnerability.

Invulnerability rests
    With self;
    Vulnerability,
    With the enemy.

The Skilful Warrior
    Can achieve
    His own
    Invulnerability;
    But he can never bring about
    The enemy's
    Vulnerability.

Hence the saying
   'One can know
   Victory
   And yet not achieve it.'

Invulnerability is
   Defence;
   Vulnerability is
   Attack.

Defence implies
   Lack;
   Attack implies
   Abundance.

A Skilful Defender
   Hides beneath
   The Ninefold Earth;
   A Skilful Attacker
   Moves above
   The Ninefold Heaven.

Thus they achieve
   Protection
And victory
   Intact.

To foresee
   The ordinary victory
   Of the common man
   Is no true skill.

To be victorious in battle
    And to be acclaimed
    For one's skill
    Is no true
    Skill.

To lift autumn fur
    Is no
    Strength;
To see sun and moon
    Is no
    Perception;
To hear thunder
    Is no
    Quickness of hearing.

The Skilful Warrior of old
    Won
    Easy victories.

The victories
    Of the Skilful Warrior
    Are not
    Extraordinary victories;
    They bring
    Neither fame for wisdom
    Nor merit for valour.

His victories
    Are
    Flawless;

His victory is
    Flawless
    Because it is
    Inevitable;
He vanquishes
    An already defeated enemy.

The Skilful Warrior
    Takes his stand
    On invulnerable ground;
    He lets slip no chance
    Of defeating the enemy.

The victorious army
    Is victorious first
    And seeks battle later;
    The defeated army
    Does battle first
    And seeks victory later.

The Skilful Strategist
    Cultivates
    The Way
    And preserves
    The law;
    Thus he is master
    Of victory and defeat.

In War,
>There are Five Steps:

>Measurement,
>Estimation,
>Calculation,
>Comparison,
>Victory.

Earth determines
>Measurement;
>Measurement determines
>Estimation;
>Estimation determines
>Calculation;
>Calculation determines
>Comparison;
>Comparison determines
>Victory.

A victorious army
>Is like a pound weight
>In the scale against
>A grain;
A defeated army
>Is like a grain
>In the scale against
>A pound weight.

A victorious army
    Is like
    Pent-up water
    Crashing
    A thousand fathoms
    Into a gorge.

This is all
    A matter of
    Forms and
    Dispositions.

Potential Energy

Master Sun said:

Managing many
    Is the same as
    Managing few;
    It is a question of
    Division.

Fighting with many
    Is the same as
    Fighting with few;
    It is a matter of
    Marshalling men
    With gongs,
    Identifying them
    With flags.

With a combination of
    Indirect and
    Direct,
    An army
    Can hold off the enemy
    Undefeated.

With an understanding of
 Weakness and
 Strength,
 An army
 Can strike
 Like a millstone
 Cast at an egg.

In warfare,
 Engage
 Directly;
 Secure victory
 Indirectly.

The warrior skilled
 In indirect warfare
 Is infinite
 As Heaven and Earth,
 Inexhaustible
 As river and sea,
 He ends and begins again
 Like sun and moon,
 Dies and is born again
 Like the Four Seasons.

There are but
 Five notes,
 And yet their permutations
 Are more
 Than can ever be heard.

There are but
    Five colours,
    And yet their permutations
    Are more
    Than can ever be seen.

There are but
    Five flavours,
    And yet their permutations
    Are more
    Than can ever be tasted.

In the dynamics of War,
    There are but these two—
    Indirect
    And direct—
    And yet their permutations
    Are inexhaustible.
    They give rise to each other
    In a never-ending,
    Inexhaustible circle.

A rushing torrent
    Carries boulders
    On its flood;
    Such is the energy
    Of its momentum.

A swooping falcon
    Breaks the back
    Of its prey;
    Such is the precision
    Of its timing.

The Skilful Warrior's energy is
    Devastating;
    His timing,
    Taut.

His energy is like
    A drawn crossbow,
    His timing like
    The release of a trigger.

In the tumult of battle,
    The struggle may seem
    Pell-mell,
    But there is no disorder;
    In the confusion of the melee,
    The battle array may seem
    Topsy-turvy,
    But defeat is out of the question.

Disorder is founded
    On order;
    Fear,
    On courage;
    Weakness,
    On strength.

Orderly disorder
    Is based on
    Careful division;
    Courageous fear,
    On potential energy;
    Strong weakness,
    On troop dispositions.

The warrior skilled at
    Stirring the enemy
    Provides a visible form,
    And the enemy is sure to come.
    He proffers the bait,
    And the enemy is sure
    To take it.
    He causes the enemy
    To make a move
    And awaits him
    With full force.

The Skilful Warrior
    Exploits
    The potential energy;
    He does not hold his men
    Responsible.
He deploys his men
    To their best
    But relies on
    The potential energy.

Relying on the energy,
    He sends his men into battle
    Like a man
    Rolling logs or boulders.
    By their nature,
    On level ground
    Logs and boulders
    Stay still;
    On steep ground
    They move;
    Square, they halt;
    Round, they roll.
    Skilfully deployed soldiers
    Are like round boulders
    Rolling down
    A mighty mountainside.

These are all matters
    Of potential energy.

Empty and Full

Master Sun said:

First on the battlefield
    Waits for the enemy
    Fresh.

Last on the battlefield
    Charges into the fray
    Exhausted.

The Skilful Warrior
    Stirs
    And is not stirred.

    He lures his enemy
    Into coming
    Or obstructs him
    From coming.

    Exhaust
    A fresh enemy;
    Starve
    A well-fed enemy;
    Unsettle
    A settled enemy.

Appear at the place
    To which he must hasten;
    Hasten to the place
    Where he least expects you.

March hundreds of miles
    Without tiring,
    By travelling
    Where no enemy is.

Be sure of victory
    By attacking
    The undefended.

Be sure of defence
    By defending
    The unattacked.

The Skilful Warrior attacks
    So that the enemy
    Cannot defend;
    He defends
    So that the enemy
    Cannot attack.

Oh, subtlety of subtleties!
    Without form!
Oh, mystery of mysteries!
    Without sound!
    He is master of
    His enemy's fate.

He advances
    Irresistibly,
    Attacking emptiness.

He retreats,
    Eluding pursuit,
    Too swift
    To be overtaken.

If I wish to engage,
    Then the enemy,
    For all his high ramparts
    And deep moat,
    Cannot avoid the engagement;
    I attack that which
    He is obliged
    To rescue.

If I do not wish to engage,
    I can hold my ground
    With nothing more than a line
    Drawn around it.
    The enemy cannot
    Engage me
    In combat:
    I distract him
    In a different direction.

His form is visible,
    But I am
    Formless;
    I am concentrated,
    He is divided.

I am concentrated
    Into one;
    He is divided
    Into ten.
    I am
    Ten
    To his one;
    Many
    Against
    His few.

Attack few with many,
    And my opponent
    Will be weak.

The place I intend to attack
    Must not be known;
    If it is unknown,
    The enemy will have to
    Reinforce many places;
    The enemy will
    Reinforce many places,
    But I shall attack
    Few.

By reinforcing his vanguard,
    He weakens his rear;
By reinforcing his rear,
    He weakens his vanguard.
By reinforcing his right flank,
    He weakens his left;
By reinforcing his left,
    He weakens his right.
By reinforcing every part,
    He weakens every part.

Weakness
    Stems from
    Preparing against attack.
Strength
    Stems from
    Obliging the enemy
    To prepare against an attack.

If we know
    The place and the day
    Of the battle,
    Then we can engage
    Even after a march
    Of hundreds of miles.

But if neither day
    Nor place
    Is known,
    Then left cannot
    Help right,

Right cannot
Help left,
Vanguard cannot
Help rear,
Rear cannot
Help vanguard.
It is still worse
If the troops
Are separated
By a dozen miles
Or even by a mile or two.

According to my assessment,
    The troops of Yue
    Are many,
    But that will avail them little
    In the struggle.
    So I say
    Victory
    Is still possible.

The enemy may be many,
    But we can prevent
    An engagement.

Scrutinize him,
    Know the flaws
    In his plans.

Rouse him,
  Discover the springs
  Of his actions.

Make his form visible,
  Discover his grounds
  Of death and life.

Probe him,
  Know his strengths
  And weaknesses.

The highest skill
  In forming dispositions
  Is to be without form;
  Formlessness
  Is proof against the prying
  Of the subtlest spy
  And the machinations
  Of the wisest brain.

Exploit the enemy's dispositions
  To attain victory;
  This the common man
  Cannot know.
  He understands
  The forms,
  The dispositions
  Of my victory;

But not
How I created the forms
Of victory.

Victorious campaigns
    Are unrepeatable.
    They take form in response
    To the infinite varieties
    Of circumstance.

Military dispositions
    Take form like water.
    Water shuns the high
    And hastens to the low.
    War shuns the strong
    And attacks the weak.

Water shapes its current
    From the lie of the land.
The warrior shapes his victory
    From the dynamic of the enemy.

War has no
    Constant dynamic;
    Water has no
    Constant form.

Supreme military skill lies
    In deriving victory
    From the changing circumstances
    Of the enemy.

Among the Five Elements
    There is no one
    Constant supremacy.
The Four Seasons
    Have no
    Fixed station;
There are long days
    And short;
    The moon
    Waxes
    And it
    Wanes.

The Fray

Master Sun said:

In War,
  The general
  Receives orders
  From his sovereign,
  Assembles troops,
  And forms an army.
  He makes camp
  Opposite the enemy.
  The true difficulty
  Begins with
  The fray itself.

The difficulty of the fray
  Lies in making
  The crooked
  Straight
  And in making
  An advantage
  Of misfortune.

Take a roundabout route,
  And lure the enemy
  With some gain;

Set out after him,
    But arrive before him;
    This is to master
    The crooked
    And the straight.

The fray can bring
    Gain;
    It can bring
    Danger.

Throw your entire force
    Into the fray
    For some gain,
    And you may still
    Fail.

Abandon camp and
    Enter the fray
    For some gain,
    And you may lose
    Your equipment.

Order your men to
    Carry their armour
    And make forced march,
    Day and night,
    Without halting,
    March thirty miles
    At double speed
    For some gain,

And you will lose
All your commanders.
The most vigorous men
Will be in the vanguard;
The weakest,
In the rear.
One in ten
Will arrive.

March fifteen miles
 For some gain,
 And the commander
 Of the vanguard
 Will fall;
 Only half the men
 Will arrive.

March ten miles
 For some gain,
 And two in three men
 Will arrive.

Without its equipment,
 An army is lost;
 Without provisions,
 An army is lost;
 Without base stores,
 An army is lost.

Without knowing the plans
>   Of the feudal lords,
>   You cannot
>   Form alliances.

Without knowing the lie
>   Of hills and woods,
>   Of cliffs and crags,
>   Of marshes and fens,
>   You cannot
>   March

Without using local guides,
>   You cannot
>   Exploit
>   The lie of the land.

War
>   Is founded
>   On deception;
>   Movement is determined
>   By advantage;
>   Division and unity
>   Are its elements
>   Of Change.

Be rushing as a wind;
>   Be stately as a forest;
Be ravaging as a fire;
>   Be still as a mountain.

Be inscrutable as night;
    Be swift as thunder or lightning.

Plunder the countryside,
    And divide the spoil;
Extend territory,
    And distribute the profits.
Weigh the situation carefully
    Before making a move.

Victory belongs to the man
    Who can master
    The stratagem of
    The crooked
    And the straight.

This is the
    Art of the Fray.

The Military Primer says:

When ears do not hear,
    Use gongs and drums.
When eyes do not see,
    Use banners and flags.

Gongs and drums,
    Banners and flags
    Are the
    Ears and eyes
    Of the army.

With the army focused,
    The brave will not
    Advance alone,
    Nor will the fearful
    Retreat alone.

This is the Art of
    Managing Many.

In night fighting,
    Use torches and drums;
In daylight,
    Use banners and flags;
    So as to transform
    The ears and eyes
    Of the troops.

A whole fighting force
    Can be robbed
    Of its spirit;
A general
    Can be robbed
    Of his presence of mind.

The soldier's spirit
    Is keenest
    In the morning;
    By noon
    It has dulled;

By evening
He has begun
To think of home.

The Skilful Warrior
   Avoids the keen spirit,
   Attacks the dull
   And the homesick;
   This is
   Mastery of Spirit.

He confronts chaos
   With discipline;
He treats tumult
   With calm.
   This is
   Mastery of Mind.

He meets distance
   With closeness;
He meets exhaustion
   With ease;
He meets hunger
   With plenty;
This is
   Mastery of Strength.

He does not intercept
   Well-ordered banners;
He does not attack
   A perfect formation.

This is
    Mastery of Change.

These are axioms
    Of the Art of War:
    Do not advance uphill.
    Do not oppose an enemy
    With his back to a hill.
    Do not pursue an enemy
    Feigning flight.
    Do not attack
    Keen troops.
    Do not swallow
    A bait.
    Do not thwart
    A returning army.

    Leave a passage
    For a besieged army.

    Do not press
    An enemy at bay.

This is
    The Art of War.

The Nine Changes

Master Sun said:

In War,
>The general
>Receives orders
>From his sovereign,
>Then assembles troops
>And forms an army.

On intractable terrain,
>Do not encamp;
On crossroad terrain,
>Join forces with allies;
On dire terrain,
>Do not linger;
On enclosed terrain,
>Make strategic plans;
On death terrain,
>Do battle.

There are roads
>Not to take.
There are armies
>Not to attack.

There are towns
    Not to besiege.
There are terrains
    Not to contest.
There are ruler's orders
    Not to obey.

The general
    Who knows the gains
    Of the Nine Changes
    Understands War.

The general
    Ignorant of the gains
    Of the Nine Changes
    May know the lie of the land,
    But he will never reap
    The gain
    Of that knowledge.

The warrior
    Ignorant of the Art
    Of the Nine Changes,
    May know
    The Five Gains
    But will not get the most
    From his men.

The wise leader
    In his deliberations
    Always blends consideration
    Of gain
    And harm.

By tempering thoughts of
    Gain,
    He can accomplish
    His goal;

By tempering thoughts of
    Harm,
    He can extricate himself
    From calamity.

He reduces the feudal lords
    To submission
    By causing them
    Harm;

He wears them down
    By keeping them
    Constantly occupied;

He precipitates them
    With thoughts of
    Gain.

The Skilful Warrior
 Does not rely on the enemy's
 Not coming,
 But on his own
 Preparedness.

He does not rely on the enemy's
 Not attacking,
 But on his own
 Impregnability.

There are Five Pitfalls
 For a general:

Recklessness,
 Leading to
 Destruction;
Cowardice,
 Leading to
 Capture;
A hot temper,
 Prone to
 Provocation;
A delicacy of honour,
 Tending to
 Shame;
A concern for his men,
 Leading to
 Trouble.

These Five Excesses
    In a general
    Are the
    Bane of war.

If an army is defeated
    And its general slain,
    It will surely be because of
    These Five Perils.
They demand the most
    Careful consideration.

On the March

Master Sun said:

In taking up position
　　And confronting the enemy:

Cross mountains,
　　Stay close to valleys;
　　Camp high,
　　And face the open;
　　Fight downhill,
　　Not up.
These are positions in
　　Mountain warfare.

Cross rivers,
　　Then keep a distance
　　From them.
　　If the enemy crosses a river
　　Towards you,
　　Do not confront him
　　In midstream.
　　Let half his troops cross
　　Before you strike.
　　If you wish to do battle,
　　Do not confront the enemy

Close to the river.
Occupy high ground,
And face the open.
Do not advance
    Against the flow.
    These are positions in
    River warfare.

Cross salt marshes
    Rapidly;
    Never linger.
    If you must do battle
    In a salt marsh,
    Keep water plants
    Close by
    And trees
    Behind you.
    These are positions in
    Salt marshes.

On level ground,
    Occupy easy terrain.
    Keep high land
    To the right and rear:
    Keep death in front
    And life to the rear.
    These are positions on
    Level ground.

Observation of
   These four types of positions
   Enabled the Yellow Emperor
   To defeat
   The Four Emperors.

Armies prize high ground,
   Shun low;
   They esteem Yang,
   Avoid Yin.

Nurture life,
   Occupy solid ground.
   Your troops will thrive,
   Victory will be sure.

On mound,
   Hill,
   Bank,
   Or dike,
   Occupy the Yang,
   With high ground
   To right and rear.
Use the lie of the land
   To the troops' benefit.

When rains upstream
   Have swollen the river,
   Let the water subside
   Before crossing.

If you come to
    Heaven's Torrents,
    Heaven's Wells,
    Heaven's Prisons,
    Heaven's Nets,
    Heaven's Traps,
    Heaven's Cracks:
    Quit such places
    With all speed.
    Do not go near them.
    Keep well away,
    Let the enemy
    Go near them.
    Keep them in front;
    Let him have them
    At his rear.

If you march by
    Ravine,
    Swamp,
    Reedy marshland,
    Mountain forest,
    Thick undergrowth:
    Beware,
    Explore them diligently.
    These are places
    Of ambush,
    Lairs for spies.

When the enemy is
　　Close at hand
　　And makes no move,
　　He is counting on
　　A strong position;

If he is
　　At a distance
　　And provokes battle,
　　He wants his opponent
　　To advance.

If he is
　　On easy ground,
　　He is luring us.

If trees move,
　　He is coming.

If there are many screens
　　In the grass,
　　He wants
　　To perplex us.

Birds rising in flight
　　Are a sign
　　Of ambush;

Beasts startled
　　Are a sign
　　Of surprise attack.

Dust high and peaking
  Is a sign
  Of chariots approaching;

Dust low and spreading
  Is a sign
  Of infantry approaching;

Dust in scattered strands
  Is a sign
  Of firewood's being collected;

Dust in drifting pockets
  Is a sign
  Of an army encamping.

Humble words, coupled with
  Increased preparations,
  Are a sign
  Of impending attack;

Strong words, coupled with
  An aggressive advance,
  Are a sign
  Of impending retreat.

Light chariots
  Emerging first
  On the wings
  Are a sign
  Of battle formation.

Words of peace,
    But no treaty,
    Are a sign
    Of a plot.

Much running about
    And soldiers parading
    Are a sign
    Of expectation.

Some men advancing
    And some retreating
    Are a sign
    Of a decoy.

Soldiers standing
    Bent on their spears
    Indicate great
    Hunger.

Bearers of water
    Drinking first
    Indicate great
    Thirst.

An advantage perceived,
    But not acted on,
    Indicates utter
    Exhaustion.

Birds gather
    On empty ground.

Shouting at night
    Is a sign
    Of fear.

Confusion among troops
    Is a sign
    That the general
    Is not respected.

Banners and flags moving
    Are a sign
    Of disorder.

If officers
    Are prone to anger,
    The men become weary.

If they feed
    Grain to their horses
    And meat to their men;
If they fail to
    Hang up their pots
    And do not
    Return to their quarters;
    Then they are
    At bay.

Men whispering together,
> Huddled in small groups,
> Are a sign
> Of disaffection.

Excessive rewards
> Are a sign
> Of desperation.

Excessive punishments
> Are a sign
> Of exhaustion.

If a general is by turns
> Tyrannical
> And in terror
> Of his own men,
> It is a sign of
> Supreme incompetence.

Envoys
> With words of conciliation
> Desire cessation.

Protracted, fierce
> Confrontation,
> With neither engagement
> Nor retreat,
> Must be regarded
> With great vigilance.

In War,
    Numbers
    Are not the issue.
It is a question of
    Not attacking
    Too aggressively.
    Concentrate your strength,
    Assess your enemy,
    And win the confidence of your men:
    That is enough.

Rashly underestimate your enemy,
    And you will surely be
    Taken captive.

Discipline troops
    Before they are loyal,
    And they will be
    Refractory
    And hard to put to good use.
    Let loyal troops
    Go undisciplined,
    And they will be altogether
    Useless.

Command them
    With civility,
    Rally them
    With martial discipline,
    And you will win their
    Confidence.

Consistent and effective orders
    Inspire obedience;
    Inconsistent and ineffective orders
    Provoke disobedience.

When orders are consistent
    And effective,
    General and troops
    Enjoy mutual trust.

Forms of Terrain

Master Sun said:

There are different forms of terrain:

> Accessible terrain,
> Entangling terrain,
> Deadlock terrain,
> Enclosed terrain,
> Precipitous terrain,
> Distant terrain.

'Accessible' means that
> Both sides
> Can come and go freely.
> On accessible terrain,
> He who occupies
> High Yang ground
> And ensures
> His line of supplies
> Will fight
> To advantage.

'Entangling' means that
> Advance is possible,
> Withdrawal hard.

On entangling terrain,
If the enemy is unprepared,
Go out and defeat him.
But if he is prepared,
And our move fails,
It will be hard to retreat.
The outcome will not be
To our advantage.

'Deadlock' means that
Neither side finds it
Advantageous
To make a move.
On deadlock terrain,
Even if our enemy
Offers a bait,
We do not make a move;
We lure him out;
We retreat.
And when half his troops
Are out,
That is our moment
To strike.

On enclosed terrain,
If we occupy it first,
We must block it
And wait for the enemy.
If he occupies it first
And blocks it,
Do not go after him;

If he does not block it,
Then go after him.

On precipitous terrain,
    If we occupy it first,
    We should hold the Yang heights
    And wait for the enemy.
    If the enemy occupies it first,
    Do not go after him,
    But entice him out
    By retreating.

On distant terrain,
    When strengths are matched,
    It is hard to provoke battle,
    And an engagement
    Will not be advantageous.

These six constitute
    The Way of Terrain.
    It is the general's duty
    To study them diligently.

In War,
    The following are not
    Natural calamities,
    But the fault
    Of the general:

Flight
Impotence,
Decay,
Collapse,
Chaos,
Rout.

If relative strengths are matched,
    But one army faces another
    Ten times its size,
    The outcome is
    Flight.

When troops are strong
    But officers weak,
    The result is
    Impotence.

When officers are strong
    But troops weak,
    The result is
    Decay.

When superior officers are angry
    And insubordinate
    And charge into battle
    Out of resentment,
    Before their general can judge
    The likelihood of victory,
    Then the outcome is
    Collapse.

When the general is weak
    And lacking in severity,
    When his orders
    Are not clear,
    When neither officers nor men
    Have fixed rules
    And troops
    Are slovenly,
    The outcome is
    Chaos.

When a general
    Misjudges his enemy
    And sends a lesser force
    Against a larger one,
    A weaker contingent
    Against a stronger one;
    When he fails to pick
    A good vanguard,
    The outcome is
    Rout.

These six constitute
    The Way of Defeat.
    It is the general's duty
    To study them diligently.

The form of the terrain
    Is the soldier's ally;

Assessment
    Of the enemy
    And mastery of victory;
    Calculating the difficulty,
    The danger,
    And the distance
    Of the terrain;
    These constitute the Way
    Of the Superior General.

He who knows this
    And practises it in battle
    Will surely be
    Victorious.
    He who does not know it
    And does not practise it
    Will surely be
    Defeated.

If an engagement is sure
    To bring victory,
    And yet the ruler
    Forbids it,
    Fight;
    If an engagement is sure
    To bring defeat,
    And yet the ruler
    Orders it,
    Do not fight.

He who advances
>Without seeking
>Fame,
>Who retreats
>Without escaping
>Blame,
>He whose one aim is
>To protect his people
>And serve his lord,
>This man is
>A Jewel of the Realm.

He regards his troops
>As his children,
>And they will go with him
>Into the deepest ravine.
>He regards them
>As his loved ones,
>And they will stand by him
>Unto death.

If he is generous
>But cannot command,
If he is affectionate
>But cannot give orders,
If he is chaotic
>And cannot keep order,
Then his men
>Will be like
>Spoiled children,
>And useless.

If we know that our own troops
>   Are capable of attacking
>   But fail to see
>   That the enemy
>   Is not vulnerable,
>   We have only
>   Half of victory.

If we know that the enemy
>   Is vulnerable
>   But fail to see
>   That our own troops
>   Are incapable of attacking,
>   We have only
>   Half of victory.

If we know that the enemy
>   Is vulnerable,
>   And know that our own troops
>   Are capable of attacking,
>   But fail to see
>   That the terrain
>   Is unfit for attack,
>   We still have only
>   Half of victory.

The Wise Warrior,
>   When he moves,
>   Is never confused;
>   When he acts,
>   Is never at a loss.

So it is said;
'Know the enemy,
Know yourself,
And victory
Is never in doubt,
Not in a hundred battles.'

Know Heaven,
Know Earth,
And your victory
Is complete.

The Nine Kinds of Ground

Master Sun said:

In War,
> There are
> Nine Kinds of Ground:

> Scattering ground,
> Light ground,
> Strategic ground,
> Open ground,
> Crossroad ground,
> Heavy ground,
> Intractable ground,
> Enclosed ground,
> Death ground.

When the feudal lords
> Fight on home territory,
> That is
> Scattering ground.

When an army enters
> Enemy territory,
> But not deeply,

That is
Light ground.

When the ground
   Offers advantage
   To either side,
   That is
   Strategic ground.

When each side
   Can come and go freely,
   That is
   Open ground.

When the ground
   Borders
   Three states
   And the first to take it
   Has mastery
   Of the empire,
   That is
   Crossroad ground.

When an army enters
   Enemy territory deeply
   And holds
   Several fortified towns
   In its rear,
   That is
   Heavy ground.

When an army travels through
    Mountains and forests,
    Cliffs and crags,
    Marshes and fens,
    Hard roads,
    These are
    Intractable ground.

Ground reached
    Through narrow gorges,
    Retreated from
    By twisting paths,
    Where a smaller force of theirs
    Can strike our larger one,
    That is
    Enclosed ground.

Ground where mere survival
    Requires
    A desperate struggle,
    Where without
    A desperate struggle
    We perish,
    That is
    Death ground.

On scattering ground,
    Do not fight.
On light ground,
    Do not halt.

On strategic ground,
    Do not attack.
On open ground,
    Do not block.
On crossroad ground,
    Form alliances.
On heavy ground,
    Plunder.
On intractable ground,
    Keep marching.
On enclosed ground,
    Devise stratagems.
On death ground,
    Fight.

The Skilful Warrior of old
    Could prevent
    The enemy's vanguard
    From linking with his rear,
    Large and small divisions
    From working together,
    Crack troops
    From helping poor troops,
    Officers and men
    From supporting one another.
    The enemy,
    Once separated,
    Could not
    Reassemble;

Once united,
Could not
Act in concert.

When there was some gain
    To be had,
    He made a move;
    When there was none,
    He halted.

To the question
    'How should we confront
    Numerous and well arrayed,
    Poised to attack?'
My reply is
    'Seize something
    He cherishes,
    And he will do your will.'

Speed
    Is the essence of War.
    Exploit the enemy's unpreparedness;
    Attack him unawares;
    Take an unexpected route.

The Way of Invasion is this:
    Deep penetration
    Brings cohesion;
    Your enemy
    Will not prevail.

Plunder fertile country
    To nourish your men.
    Cherish your troops,
    Do not wear them out.
    Nurture your energy;
    Concentrate it.

Move your men about;
    Devise stratagems
    That cannot be fathomed.
    Throw your men
    Where there is no escape,
    And they will die
    Rather than flee.
    Men who have
    Faced death
    Can achieve anything;
    They will give
    Their last drop of strength,
    Officers and men alike.

Troops in desperate straits
    Know no fear.
    Where there is no escape,
    They stand firm;
    When they have entered deep,
    They persist;
    When they see no hope,
    They fight.

They are alert
    Without needing
    Discipline;
    They act
    Without needing
    Instructions;
    They are devoted
    Without needing
    A compact;
    They are loyal
    Without needing
    Orders.

Forbid the consulting of omens,
    Cast out doubts,
    And they will go on
    To the death.

Our men have no excess
    Of worldly goods,
    And yet they do not
    Disdain wealth;
    They do not expect
    To live long,
    And yet they do not
    Disdain long life.

On the day
    They are ordered into battle,
    They sit up and weep,
    Wetting their clothes with their tears;

They lie down and weep,
Wetting their cheeks.

But throw them
    Where there is no escape,
    And they will fight
    With the courage
    Of the heroes
    Zhu and Gui.

The Skilful Warrior
    Deploys his troops
    Like the *shuairan* snake
    Found on Mount Heng.
    Strike its head,
    And the tail lashes back;
    Strike its tail,
    And the head fights back;
    Strike its belly,
    And both head and tail
    Will attack you.
    To the question
    'Can an army be
    Like the *shuairan* snake?'
    I reply,
    'Yes, it can.'
    Take the men of Wu
    And the men of Yue.
    They are enemies,
    But if they cross a river
    In the same boat

And encounter a wind,
They will help each other,
Like right hand and left.

It is not enough
    To tether horses
    And to bury
    Chariot wheels.

There must be a single courage
    Throughout:
    This is the Way
    To manage an Army.

Strong and weak,
    Both can serve,
    Thanks to the principle
    Of ground.

The Skilful Warrior
    Directs his army
    As if it were
    A single man.
    He leaves it no choice
    But to obey.

It is the business of the general
    To be still
    And inscrutable,
    To be upright
    And impartial.

He must be able
    To keep his own troops
    In ignorance,
    To deceive their eyes
    And their ears.

He changes his ways
    And alters his plans
    To keep the enemy
    In ignorance.

He shifts camp
    And takes roundabout routes
    To keep the enemy
    In the dark.

He leads his men into battle
    Like a man
    Climbing a height
    And kicking away the ladder;
    He leads them
    Deep into the territory
    Of the feudal lords
    And releases the trigger.
    He burns his boats,
    He breaks his pots.
    He is like a shepherd
    Driving his sheep
    This way and that;
    No one knows
    Where he is going.

He assembles his troops
    And throws them
    Into danger;
    This is the business
    Of the commander.

These things must be studied:
    The Variations
    Of the Nine Kinds of Ground;
    The Advantages
    Of Flexible Manouvre;
    The Principles
    Of Human Nature.

The Way of Invasion is this:
    Deep penetration
    Brings cohesion;
    Shallow penetration
    Brings scattering.

When you leave your own territory
    And lead your men
    Across the border,
    You enter dire terrain.

When there are lines of communication
    On all four sides,
    You are on
    Crossroad terrain.

When you penetrate deeply,
>You are on
>Heavy terrain.

When you penetrate superficially,
>You are on
>Light terrain.

When there are strongholds to your rear
>And narrow passes in front,
>You are on
>Enclosed terrain.

When there is no way out,
>You are on
>Death terrain.

On scattering ground,
>We unite the will of our men.

On light ground,
>We keep them connected.

On strategic ground,
>We bring up our rear.

On open ground,
>We see to our defences.

On crossroad ground,
>We strengthen our alliances.

On heavy ground,
      We ensure continuity of supplies.

On intractable ground,
      We keep on the move.

On enclosed ground,
      We block the passes.

On death ground,
      We demonstrate
      The desperateness
      Of the situation.

It is in the soldier's nature that
      When surrounded,
      He resists;
      When all seems lost,
      He struggles on;
      When in danger,
      He obeys orders.

Without knowing the plans
      Of the feudal lords,
      You cannot
      Form alliances.

Without knowing the lie
      Of hills and woods,
      Of cliffs and crags,
      Of marshes and fens,

You cannot
    March.

Without using local guides,
    You cannot
    Exploit
    The lie of the land.

Ignorance of any one
    Of these points
    Is not characteristic
    Of the army of a great king.

When the army of a great king
    Attacks a powerful state,
    He does not allow the enemy
    To concentrate his forces.
    He overawes the enemy
    And undermines his alliances.

He does not strive
    To ally himself
    With all the other states;
He does not foster
    Their power;
He pursues
    His own secret designs,
    Overawing his enemies.

Thus he can capture
    The enemy's cities
    And destroy
    The enemy's state.

Distribute rewards
    Without undue respect for rules;
    Publish orders
    Without undue regard for precedent;

Deal with a whole army
    As if it were a single man.
    Apply them to their task
    Without words of explanation.
    Confront them with the advantage,
    But do not explain the danger.

Throw them into
    Perilous ground,
    And they will survive;
    Plunge them into
    Death ground,
    And they will live.

When a force
    Has fallen into danger,
    It can
    Snatch victory
    From defeat.

Success in war
    Lies in
    Scrutinizing
    Enemy intentions.
    And going with them.

Focus on the enemy,
    And from hundreds of miles
    You can kill their general.
    This is
    Success
    Through cunning.

On the day
    You decide to attack,
    Close the passes,
    Destroy the tallies,
    Break off intercourse
    With envoys;
    Be firm in the temple council
    For the execution of
    Your plans.

If the enemy opens a door,
    Rush in.
    Seize what he holds dear,
    And secretly contrive
    An encounter.

Discard rules,
    Follow the enemy,
    To fight
    The decisive battle.

At first,
    Be like a maiden;
    When the enemy opens the door,
    Be swift as a hare;
    Your enemy will not
    Withstand you.

Attack by Fire

Master Sun said:

> There are Five Ways to
> Attack by Fire.
>
> The first is to burn
> Men;
>
> The second is to burn
> Supplies;
>
> The third is to burn
> Equipment;
>
> The fourth is to burn
> Warehouses;
>
> The fifth is to burn
> Lines of communication.

Attack by fire
> Requires means;
> The material
> Must be ready.

There is a season
    For making a fire;
    There are days
    For lighting a flame.

The proper season is
    When the weather is
    Hot and dry;

The proper days are
    When the moon is in
    Sagittarius,
    Pegasus,
    Crater,
    Corvus.
    These are the
    Four Constellations
    Of Rising Wind.

When attacking with fire,
    Adapt to
    These Five Changes of Fire:

If fire breaks out
    Within the enemy camp,
    Respond at once
    From without.

If fire breaks out
    But the enemy remains calm,
    Wait,
    Do not attack.
    Let the fire reach
    Its height,
    And follow up
    If at all possible;
    If not,
    Wait.

If fire attack is possible
    From without,
    Do not wait
    For fire to be started
    Within;
    Light
    When the time is right.

When starting a fire,
    Be upwind;
    Never attack
    From downwind.

A wind that rises
    During the day
    Lasts long;
    A night wind
    Soon fails.

In War,
> Know these
> Five Changes of Fire,
> And be vigilant.

Fire
> Assists an attack
> Mightily.

Water
> Assists an attack
> Powerfully.

Water
> Can isolate,
> But it cannot
> Take away.

To win victory,
> To complete an objective,
> But not to follow through,
> Is a disastrous
> Waste.

Hence the saying
> 'The enlightened ruler
> Considers deeply;
> The effective general
> Follows through.'

Never move
  Except for gain;
Never deploy
  Except for victory;
Never fight
  Except in a crisis.

A ruler
  Must never
  Mobilize his men
  Out of anger;
  A general
  Must never
  Engage battle
  Out of spite.

Move
  If there is gain;
Halt
  If there is no gain.

Anger
  Can turn to
  Pleasure;
Spite
  Can turn to
  Joy.
But a nation destroyed
  Cannot be
  Put back together again;

A dead man
Cannot be
Brought back to life.

So the enlightened ruler
    Is prudent;
The effective general
    Is cautious.
This is the Way
    To keep a nation
    At peace
    And an army
    Intact.

Espionage

Master Sun said:

> Raising an army
> Of a hundred thousand men
> And marching them
> Three hundred miles
> Drains the pockets
> Of the common people
> And the public treasury
> To the daily sum of
> A thousand taels of silver.
> It causes commotion
> At home and abroad
> And sets countless men
> Tramping the highways
> Exhausted.
> It keeps seven hundred thousand families
> From their work.

Two armies may
> Confront each other
> For several years,
> For a single
> Decisive battle.

It is callous
> To begrudge the expense of
> A hundred taels
> Of silver
> For knowledge
> Of the enemy's situation.

Such a miser is
> No commander of men,
> No support to his lord,
> No master of victory.

Prior information
> Enables wise rulers
> And worthy generals
> To move
> And conquer,
> Brings them success
> Beyond that of the multitude.

This information
> Cannot be obtained
> From spirits;
> It cannot be deduced
> By analogy;
> It cannot be calculated
> By measurement.

It can be obtained only
> From men,
> From those who know
> The enemy's dispositions.

There are Five Sorts of Spies:

> Local,
> Internal,
> Double,
> Dead, and
> Live.

When these five sorts of espionage
> Are in operation,
> No one knows
> The Way of it.
> It is called
> The Mysterious Skein,
> The Lord's Treasure.

Local spies
> Come from among our enemy's
> Fellow countrymen;

Internal spies,
> From among our enemy's
> Officials,

Double spies,
    From among our enemy's
    Own spies.

Dead spies
    Are those for whom
    We deliberately create
    False information;
    They then pass it on
    To the enemy.

Live spies
    Are those who return
    With information.

In the whole army,
    None should be closer
    To the commander
    Than his spies,
    None more highly rewarded,
    None more confidentially treated.

Without wisdom,
    It is impossible
    To employ spies.

Without humanity and justice,
    It is impossible
    To employ spies.

Without subtlety and ingenuity,
    It is impossible
    To ascertain
    The truth of their reports.

Subtlety of subtleties!
    Spies have
    Innumerable uses.

If confidential information
    Is prematurely divulged,
    Both spy and recipient
    Must be put to death.

In striking an army,
    In attacking a city,
    In killing an individual,
    It is necessary to know beforehand
    The names of the general
    And of his attendants,
    His aides,
    His doorkeepers,
    His bodyguards.
    Our spies must be instructed
    To discover all of these
    In detail.

Enemy spies,
    Come to spy on us,
    Must be sought out,
    Bribed,

Won over,
Well accommodated.
Then they can be
Employed as
Double agents.

From the double agent
    We discover
    Local and internal spies.

From the double agent
    We learn how best
    To convey misinformation
    To the enemy.

From the double agent
    We know how and when
    To use
    Live spies.

The ruler
    Must know all five of these
    Sorts of spies;
    This knowledge must come
    From the double agent;
    So the double agent
    Must be
    Treated generously.

Of old,
    The rise of the Yin dynasty
    Was due to Yi Zhi,
    Who had served under the Xia;
    And the rise of the Zhou dynasty
    Was due to Lü Ya,
    Who had served under the Yin.

Only the enlightened ruler,
    The worthy general,
    Can use
    The highest intelligence
    For spying,
    Thereby achieving
    Great success.

Spies
    Are a key element
    In warfare.
    On them depends
    An army's
    Every move.

read more

PENGUIN CLASSICS

CITY OF GOD
ST AUGUSTINE

> 'The Heavenly City outshines Rome, beyond comparison.
> There, instead of victory, is truth; instead of rank, holiness'

St Augustine, bishop of Hippo, was one of the central figures in the history of
Christianity, and *City of God* is one of his greatest theological works. Written as an
eloquent defence of the faith at a time when the Roman Empire was on the brink
of collapse, it examines the ancient pagan religions of Rome, the arguments of the
Greek philosophers and the revelations of the Bible. Pointing the way forward to
a citizenship that transcends the best political experiences of the world and offers
citizenship that will last for eternity, *City of God* is one of the most influential
documents in the development of Christianity.

This edition contains a new introduction that examines the text in the light of
contemporary Greek and Roman thought and political change, and demonstrates
the religious and literary influences on St Augustine and his significance as a
Christian thinker. There is also a chronology and bibliography.

Translated with notes by Henry Bettenson with an introduction by Gill Evans

PENGUIN CLASSICS

THE BOOK OF CHUANG ZHU
CHUANG ZHU

'Walk with Virtue and travel with the Tao, and you will reach the perfect end'

One of the great founders of Taoism, Chuang Tzu lived in the fourth century BC and is one of the most intriguing and entertaining of Chinese philosophers. He was firmly opposed to Confucian values of order, control and hierarchy, believing the perfect state to be one where primal, innate nature rules. *The Book of Chuang Tzu* perceives the Tao – the Way of Nature – not as a term to be explained but as a path to walk; a journey towards the edge of reality, and beyond to the world of nature. Radical and subversive, employing wit, humour and shock tactics, *The Book of Chuang Tzu* is concerned not with government but with life and growth of the individual spirit.

Martin Palmer's lyrical translation conveys the passion and tone of Chuang Tzu's writing, while his introduction places Chuang Tzu's ideas and terminology in context, and discusses his key themes. This edition also includes an Index to the text.

Translated by Martin Palmer with Elizabeth Breuilly
With an introduction by Martin Palmer

THE STORY OF PENGUIN CLASSICS

Before 1946 ... 'Classics' are mainly the domain of academics and students; readable editions for everyone else are almost unheard of. This all changes when a little-known classicist, E. V. Rieu, presents Penguin founder Allen Lane with the translation of Homer's *Odyssey* that he has been working on in his spare time.

1946 Penguin Classics debuts with *The Odyssey*, which promptly sells three million copies. Suddenly, classics are no longer for the privileged few.

1950s Rieu, now series editor, turns to professional writers for the best modern, readable translations, including Dorothy L. Sayers's *Inferno* and Robert Graves's unexpurgated *Twelve Caesars*.

1960s The Classics are given the distinctive black covers that have remained a constant throughout the life of the series. Rieu retires in 1964, hailing the Penguin Classics list as 'the greatest educative force of the twentieth century.'

1970s A new generation of translators swells the Penguin Classics ranks, introducing readers of English to classics of world literature from more than twenty languages. The list grows to encompass more history, philosophy, science, religion and politics.

1980s The Penguin American Library launches with titles such as *Uncle Tom's Cabin*, and joins forces with Penguin Classics to provide the most comprehensive library of world literature available from any paperback publisher.

1990s The launch of Penguin Audiobooks brings the classics to a listening audience for the first time, and in 1999 the worldwide launch of the Penguin Classics website extends their reach to the global online community.

The 21st Century Penguin Classics are completely redesigned for the first time in nearly twenty years. This world-famous series now consists of more than 1300 titles, making the widest range of the best books ever written available to millions – and constantly redefining what makes a 'classic'.

The Odyssey continues ...

The best books ever written

PENGUIN 🐧 CLASSICS

SINCE 1946

Find out more at www.penguinclassics.com